The Flying Fish

Story by Annette Smith
Illustrations by Paul Könye

"It's Kite Day on Sunday," said Alex.

"Are you coming, Jonathan?

I'm getting a new kite.

My dad's going to buy it for me."

"I don't have a kite,"

Jonathan said sadly.

"Dad," said Jonathan,

"can you buy me a kite

to take to the park on Sunday?

Alex is going.

He is taking his new kite."

Dad smiled at Jonathan.

"I can **make** kites," he said.

"Come and look at this,"
said Dad. "Here's a good kite."

"Yes!" said Jonathan.
"It looks like a fish.
Can we make that one?"

He went to get some paper.

Jonathan and Dad made the kite.

1

2

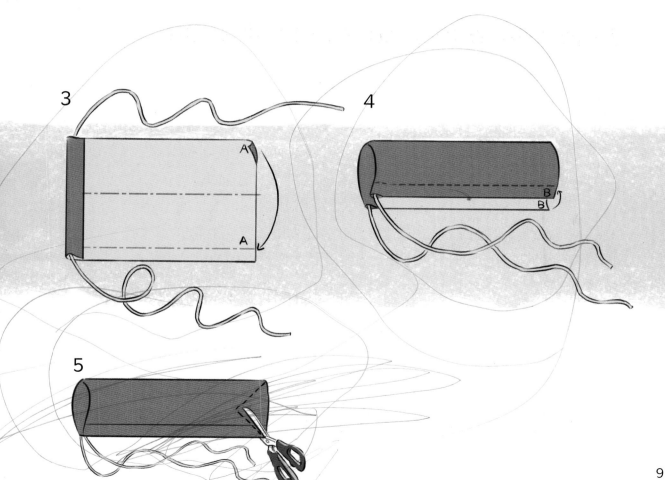

3

4

5

Jonathan cut the tail.

Then, he made some fins,

and some round spots

and two big eyes.

"My kite looks like a fish now,"

said Jonathan,

"and it can open its mouth!"

Dad helped Jonathan
to fix the string.

Then, they tied the string
to a long stick.

On Kite Day, Jonathan and Dad walked up to the park.

Alex saw Jonathan.

"I like your kite," he said.

"It looks like a fish."

"It's a **flying** fish," said Jonathan.

"My dad helped me make it."

"Come on," said Alex.

"Let's fly our kites."